HOW TO MEASURE Temperature

Darice Bailer

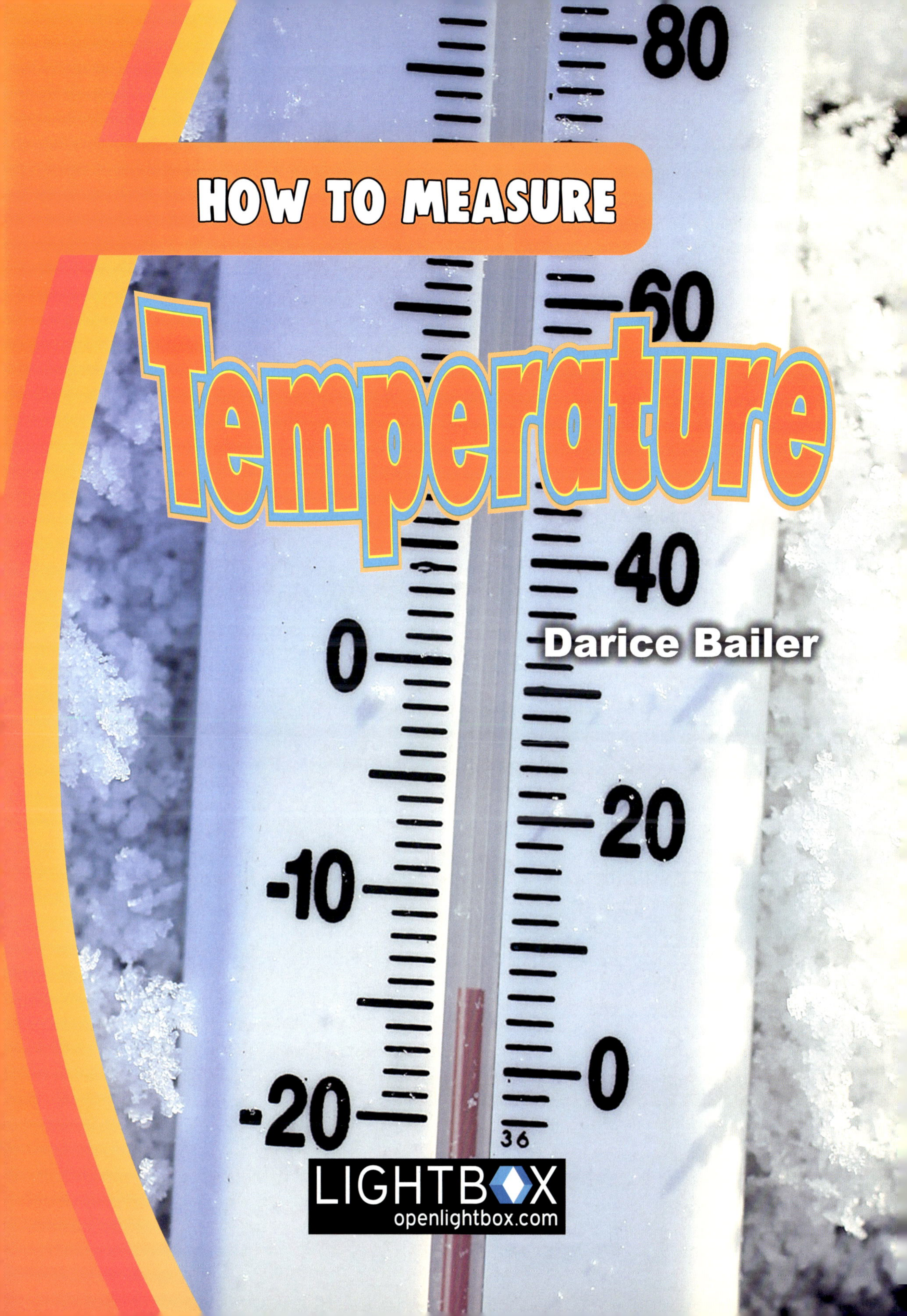

LIGHTBOX
openlightbox.com

Lightbox is an all-inclusive digital solution for the teaching and learning of curriculum topics in an original, groundbreaking way. Lightbox is based on National Curriculum Standards.

STANDARD FEATURES OF LIGHTBOX

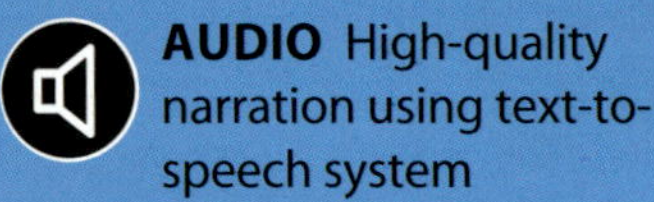
AUDIO High-quality narration using text-to-speech system

ACTIVITIES Printable PDFs that can be emailed and graded

SLIDESHOWS Pictorial overviews of key concepts

VIDEOS Embedded high-definition video clips

WEBLINKS Curated links to external, child-safe resources

TRANSPARENCIES Step-by-step layering of maps, diagrams, charts, and timelines

INTERACTIVE MAPS Interactive maps and aerial satellite imagery

QUIZZES Ten multiple choice questions that are automatically graded and emailed for teacher assessment

KEY WORDS Matching key concepts to their definitions

Contents

Lightbox Access Code 2

What Is Temperature?..........4

Temperature Timeline...........7

A Measure of Degrees 8

Two Ways to Measure...... 12

Boiling and Freezing 16

Record-Setting Temperatures 20

Quiz 22

Key Words / Index 23

www.openlightbox.com ... 24

What Is Temperature?

Many pets need their owners to control how hot or cold their tank is. This includes fish and reptiles, such as snakes and lizards.

It's your birthday. A friend gave you a fish tank. It has an orange fish. Make sure the water isn't too hot or cold!

A fish's body is as cool as the water it lives in.

You can dip a finger in the water and see. But you'd only be guessing the **temperature**.

You need a **thermometer**! This tool measures temperature.

Temperature is how hot things are. The word *thermometer* means "to measure heat."

You can measure the temperature outside. You can check it in a glass of milk. Let's measure temperature!

To do the activities in this book, you will need:

- instant-read thermometer (Note: You can find one at a grocery or hardware store.)
- piece of heavy paper
- paper fastener
- black and red markers
- scissors
- pencil

Temperature Timeline

1500s The first thermometers, called thermoscopes, are made. With a thermoscope, people cannot tell the exact temperature. They can only see a change in temperature.

1700s Scientists in Europe make many improvements to thermometers. Thermometers now give exact temperatures.

1866 A doctor in Great Britain invents a 6-inch (15-centimeter) thermometer for sick people. It takes 5 minutes to read someone's temperature.

1984 Scientists invent the ear thermometer. These thermometers become very popular. They are easy to use on babies and children.

2011 The United States Department of Agriculture (USDA) updates its food temperature guidelines. People are advised to use a thermometer when cooking meat.

2016–2017 The National Aeronautics and Space Administration (NASA) reports that August 2016 and August 2017 are the first and second hottest months ever recorded.

A Measure of Degrees

Candy thermometers were invented in Germany in the 1200s. They are used for making candy, jams, and jellies.

There are many kinds of thermometers. Ivy is making fudge. She uses a candy thermometer. These are usually glass. They have colored liquid inside. The liquid rises as the fudge gets hotter. The thermometer shows when the fudge is the right temperature.

Use a **digital** thermometer when you are sick. It beeps and shows you your temperature!

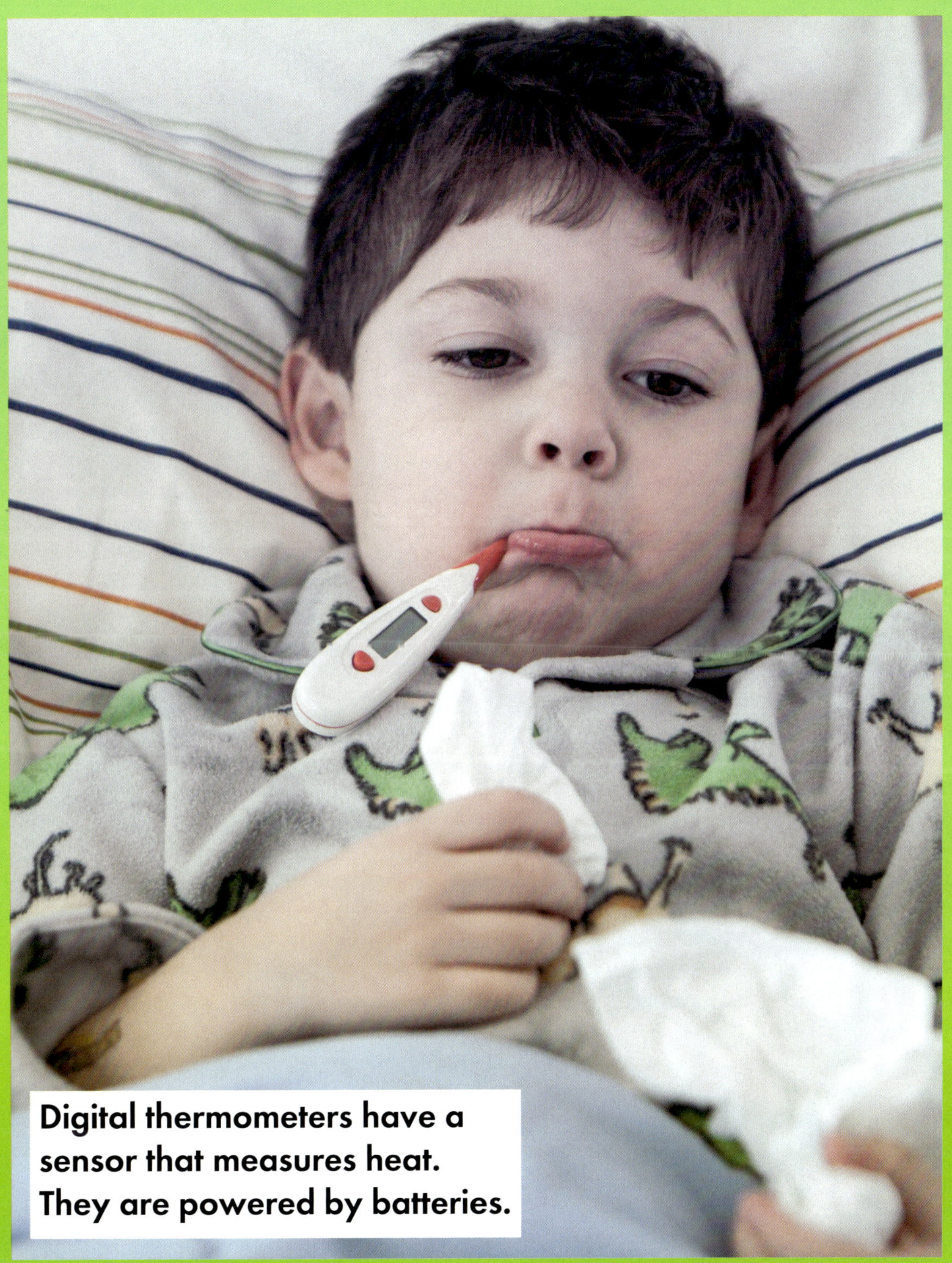

Digital thermometers have a sensor that measures heat. They are powered by batteries.

Thermometers measure heat in **degrees**. A degree is a **unit** for measuring heat.

Numbers go from low to high. A frosty glass of milk has a low number, or temperature. Hot chocolate has a higher temperature.

A hot drink does not raise your body temperature. But it can make your hands, mouth, and throat feel warmer.

Activity

Make a Pretend Thermometer!

Instructions:

1. Trace around a small plate on the heavy paper.
2. Cut out the circle.
3. Count from 0 to 220 by 20s and write the numbers around the circle. Use the black marker.
4. Add three tick marks between each number. Each tick mark is 5 degrees. The tick marks count degrees by 5s.
5. Draw an arrow on the leftover paper. Cut out the arrow. Color it red.
6. Take out the paper fastener. Fasten the arrow in the middle of your thermometer.

Two Ways to Measure

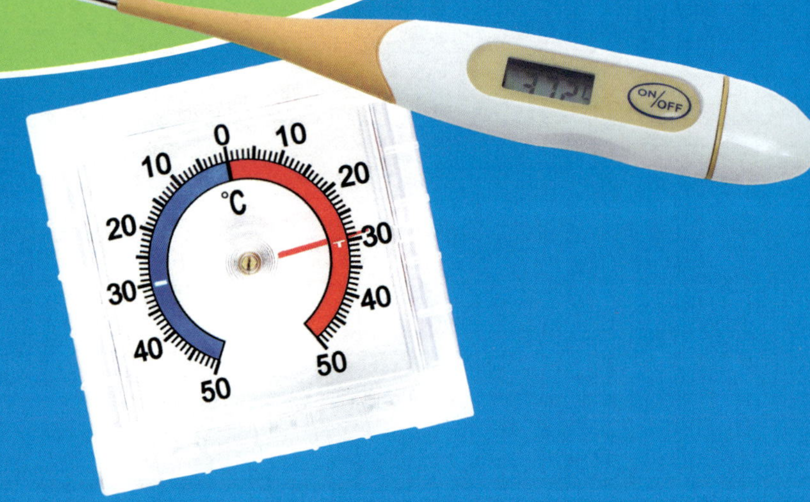

Many thermometers have two sets of numbers. They measure two different ways. One set says °F. The other says °C.

Many thermometers are filled with a colored liquid. The liquid is called ethanol and is made from plants.

The circle means "degrees." The F stands for degrees **Fahrenheit**. Fahrenheit is a **scale** in the **U.S. customary system**. People in the United States usually use this system.

The C stands for degrees **Celsius**. Celsius is a scale in the **metric system**. People in many other countries use this system. Scientists do, too!

The scientific study of heat is called thermodynamics.

Ivy and Max are on a scavenger hunt. They are hunting for thermometers around the house!

Ivy finds one outside the kitchen window. It is a weather thermometer. It shows how hot it is outside.

Max finds a **thermostat** on the wall. That shows the temperature of the room.

Experts suggest people keep their houses at about 68°F (20°C) in the winter and 78°F (26°C) in the summer.

Activity

Practice Measuring Temperature

Instructions:

1 Pour a glass of milk. Stick your instant-read thermometer in the glass. Does your thermometer measure in Fahrenheit, Celsius, or both?

2 Wait one minute. What is the milk's temperature? Take your paper thermometer from the first activity. The paper thermometer shows degrees Fahrenheit. Move the arrow to show the milk's temperature.

3 Next, scoop ice cream into a bowl. Poke the thermometer into the ice cream. What happens to the temperature? Move the arrow on your paper thermometer.

4 Now ask an adult to make you a cup of hot chocolate. Stick the thermometer in the hot chocolate. What happens now? Move the arrow on your paper thermometer.

5 Enjoy your milk, ice cream, and hot chocolate!

Boiling and Freezing

At what temperature does water freeze and turn to ice? At what temperature does water boil? Time to experiment and see!

Ivy drops some ice cubes into a cup. Max's mom boils a pot of water on the stove.

There are actually nine different types of ice. The ice people use at home is known as Ice I.

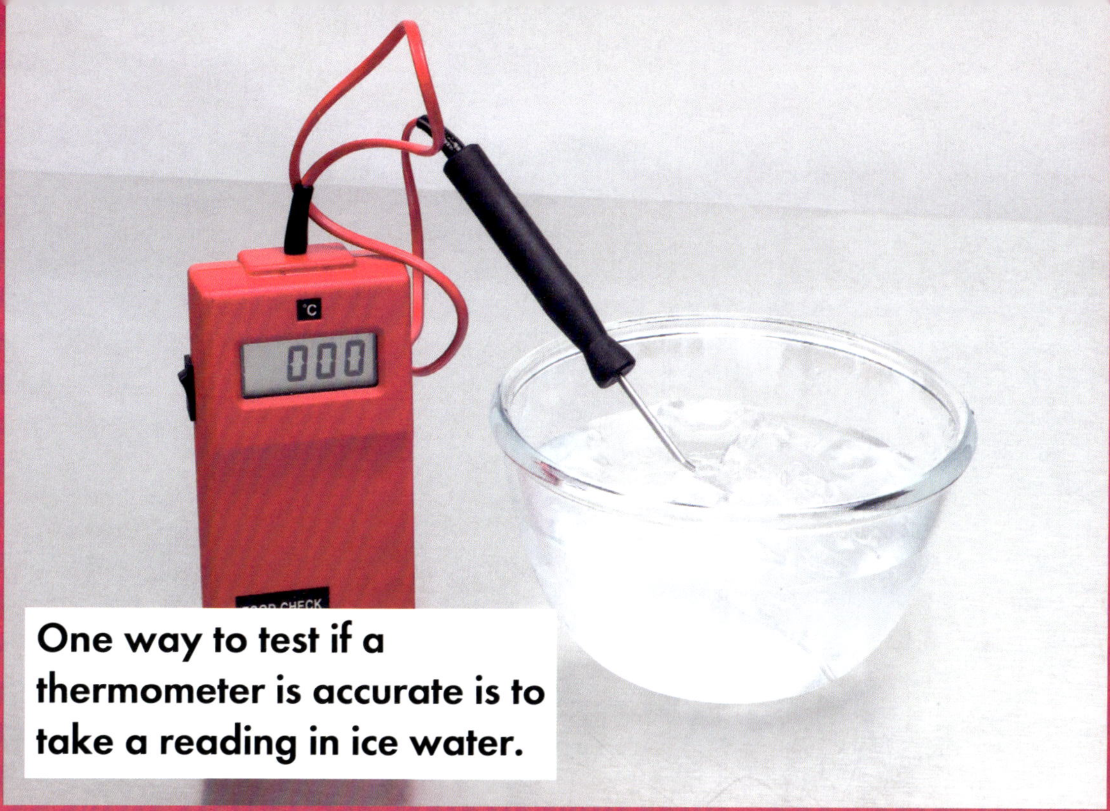

One way to test if a thermometer is accurate is to take a reading in ice water.

Ivy pokes her instant-read thermometer into the ice. The thermometer drops. It falls to 30 degrees Fahrenheit. Water turns to ice at 32 degrees Fahrenheit. That is the same as 0 degrees Celsius.

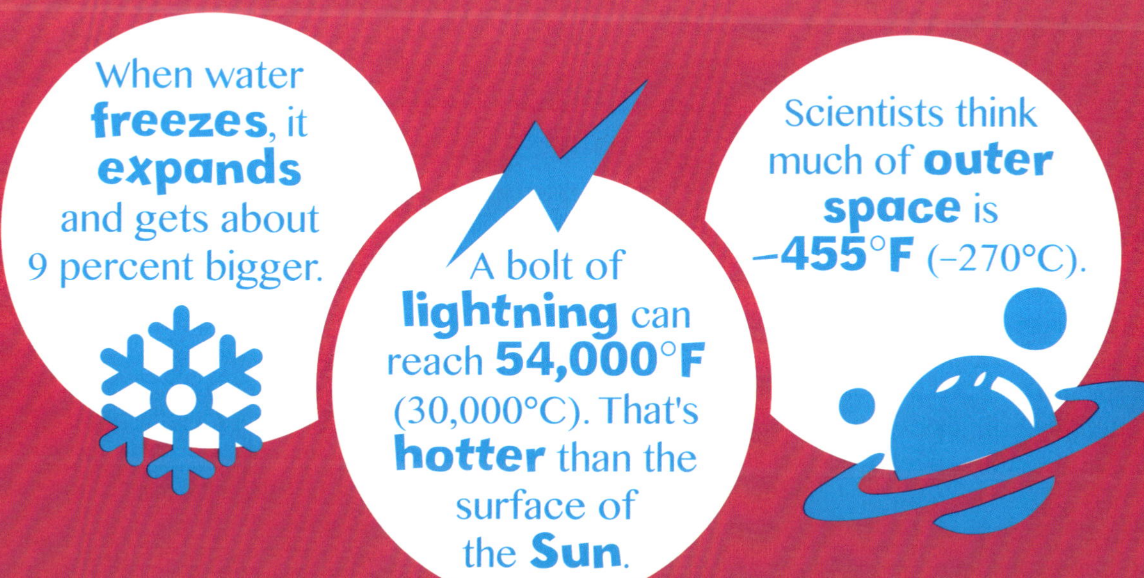

Putting a lid on a pot traps heat and raises the temperature. This makes water boil more quickly.

Max's mom puts on a mitt. She sticks the thermometer in the pot. The numbers climb higher. The thermometer reads 212 degrees Fahrenheit. That's the same as 100 degrees Celsius. Water boils at that temperature.

Activity

Guess the Temperature!

Instructions:

1. Pour a glass of cold water from the faucet.
2. What do you think the temperature will be? Is it higher than 32 degrees Fahrenheit or lower? Why?
3. Now measure the temperature with your instant-read thermometer. How close was your guess?
4. Fill up the bathtub with warm water. What do you think the temperature will be? Is it higher than 212 degrees Fahrenheit or lower? Why?
5. Now measure it. How close was your guess?

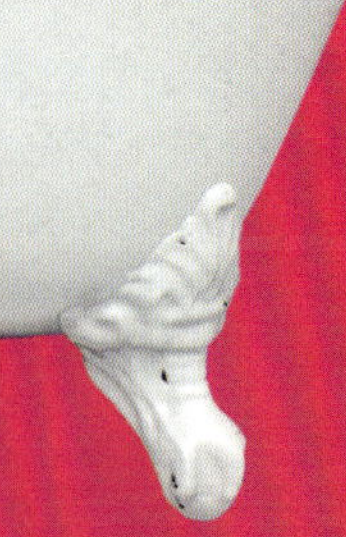

Bath water has to be comfortable but hot enough to wash away dirt and bacteria. Scientists recommend a temperature of 112°F (44°C).

Record-Setting Temperatures

There are many record-setting temperatures in the United States. Some of these are the hottest or coldest in the nation, or even in the world.

Death Valley National Park
California and Nevada

The record for hottest temperature in the United States was taken in Death Valley. On July 10, 1913, it was 134°F (57°C).

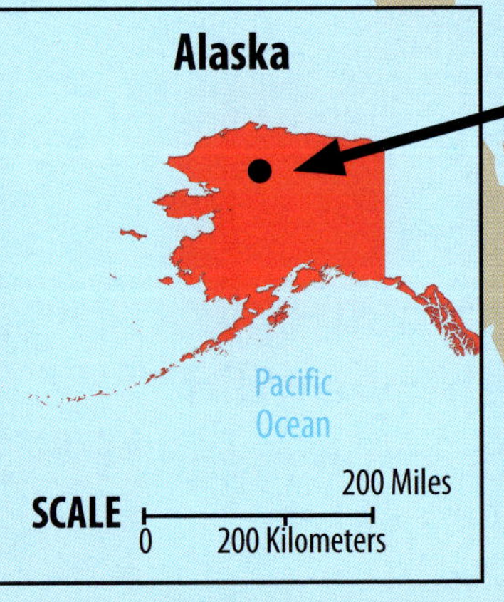

Prospect Creek
Alaska

The coldest temperature on record for the United States is –80°F (–62°C). It was taken on January 23, 1971, in Alaska.

Oklahoma City
Oklahoma

On the afternoon of November 11, 1911, in Oklahoma City, it was 83°F (28°C). By midnight, it was 17°F (–8°C). That's a U.S. record drop of 66°F (19°C) in one day.

Brookhaven National Laboratory
Upton, New York

During an experiment, scientists in the Brookhaven National Laboratory measured temperatures of 7.2 trillion°F (4 trillion°C). That's the hottest temperature ever created by humans.

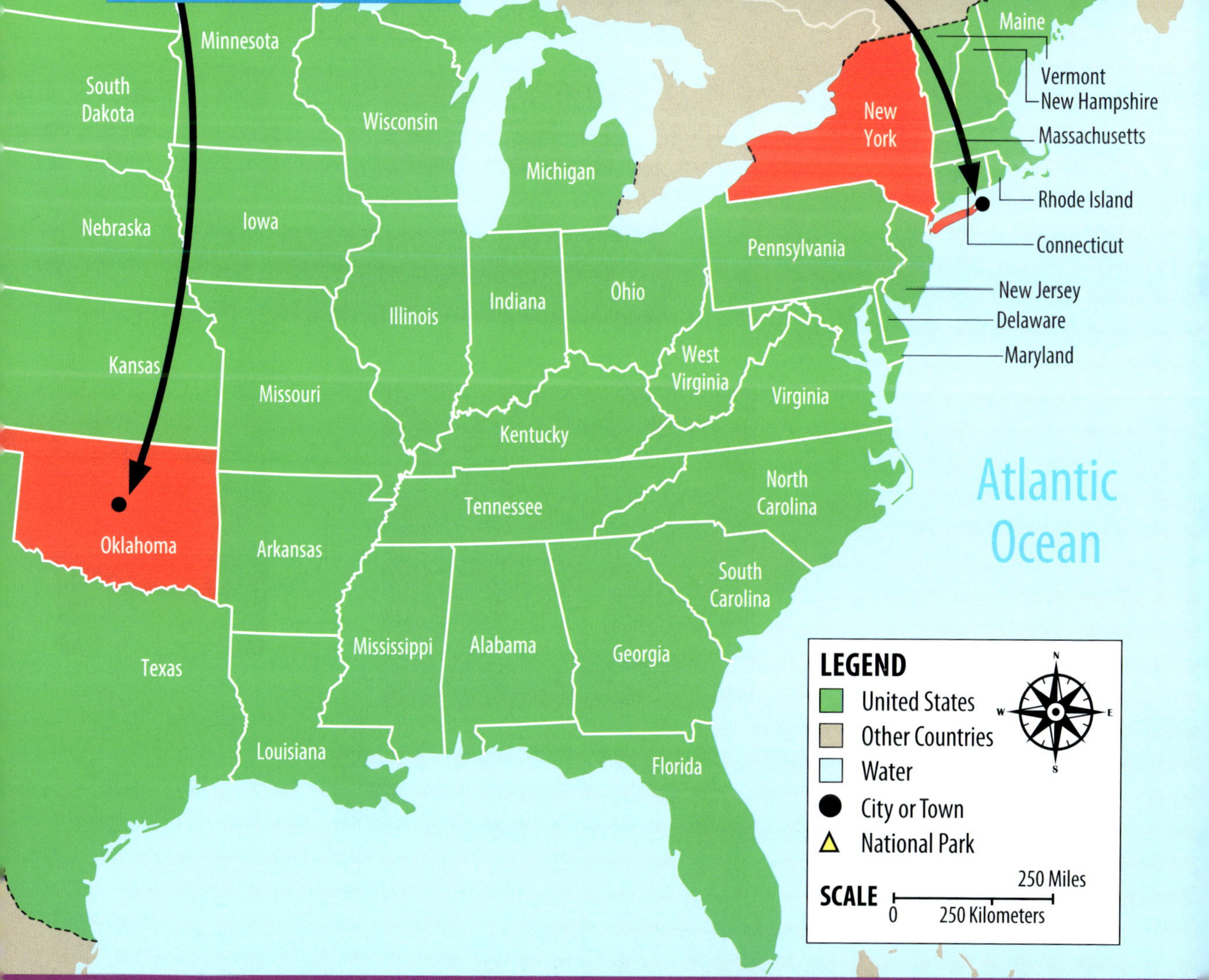

North Dakota
South Dakota
Minnesota
Wisconsin
Michigan
Nebraska
Iowa
Illinois
Indiana
Ohio
Pennsylvania
New York
Maine
Vermont
New Hampshire
Massachusetts
Rhode Island
Connecticut
New Jersey
Delaware
Maryland
Kansas
Missouri
West Virginia
Virginia
Kentucky
Oklahoma
Arkansas
Tennessee
North Carolina
South Carolina
Texas
Mississippi
Alabama
Georgia
Louisiana
Florida
Atlantic Ocean

LEGEND

- United States
- Other Countries
- Water
- City or Town
- National Park

SCALE 0 — 250 Miles — 250 Kilometers

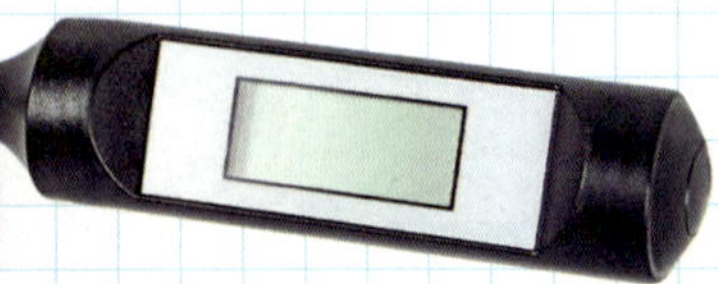

1 What tool measures temperature?

2 When were the first thermometers made?

3 When was the first medical thermometer made?

4 What unit do thermometers use to measure heat?

5 What degree system do people in the United States use?

6 What does C stand for?

7 What shows the temperature of a room?

8 At what temperature does water turn to ice?

9 At what temperature does water boil?

10 Where was the hottest temperature in the United States taken?

Answers: 1. A thermometer **2.** The 1500s **3.** 1866 **4.** Degrees **5.** Fahrenheit **6.** Celsius **7.** A thermostat **8.** 32°F (0°C) **9.** 212°F (100°C) **10.** Death Valley

Key Words

Celsius: one way of measuring temperature; water freezes at 0 degrees and boils at 100 degrees Celsius

degrees: units, or numbers, for measuring temperature

digital: showing temperature (or time, or speed) in numbers

Fahrenheit: one way of measuring temperature; water freezes at 32 degrees and boils at 212 degrees Fahrenheit

metric system: a way to measure things based on the number ten; degrees Celsius are used to measure temperature

scale: a series of numbers used to measure something

temperature: how hot something is

thermometer: a tool used to measure temperature

thermostat: tool that tells the temperature inside a room; you can set the thermostat to a certain temperature, too

unit: a standard amount used to measure something

U.S. customary system: units of measurement typically used in the United States such as degrees Fahrenheit, cups, quarts, miles, feet, and inches

boiling 16, 18, 22

Celsius 12, 13, 15, 17, 18, 22
cold 4, 5, 19, 20

degrees 10, 11, 13, 15, 17, 18, 19, 22

Fahrenheit 12, 13, 15, 17, 18, 19, 22
freezing 16, 17

guessing 5, 19

hot 4, 5, 6, 7, 8, 10, 14, 15, 19, 20, 21, 22

ice 16, 17, 22

measure 5, 6, 9, 10, 12, 15, 19, 22
metric system 13

outside 6, 14

thermometers 5, 6, 7, 8, 9, 10, 11, 12, 14, 15, 17, 18, 19, 22
thermostats 14, 22

units 10, 22
U.S. customary system 13

water 4, 5, 16, 17, 18, 19, 22

LIGHTBOX

SUPPLEMENTARY RESOURCES

Click on the plus icon found in the bottom left corner of each spread to open additional teacher resources.

- Download and print the book's quizzes and activities
- Access curriculum correlations
- Explore additional web applications that enhance the Lightbox experience

LIGHTBOX DIGITAL TITLES

Packed full of integrated media

VIDEOS

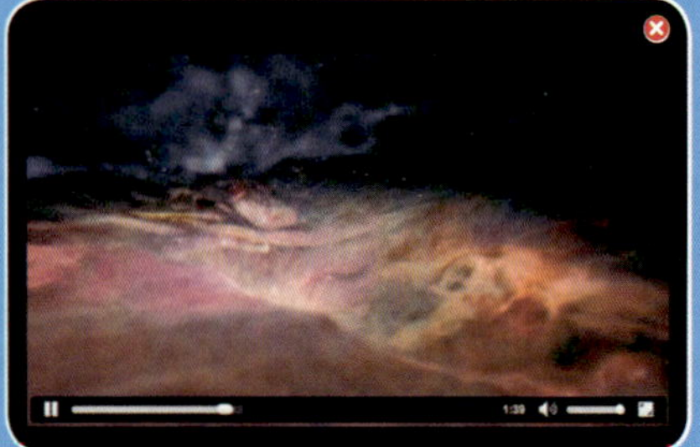

INTERACTIVE MAPS

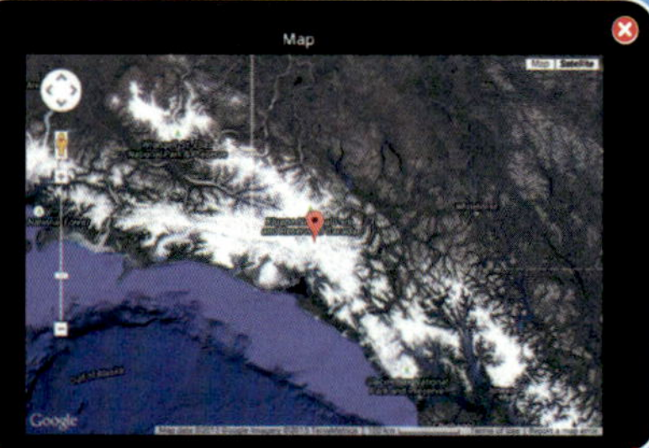

WEBLINKS

SLIDESHOWS

QUIZZES

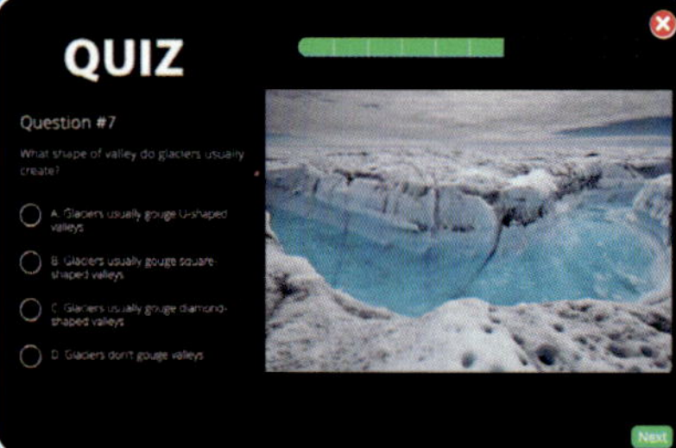

OPTIMIZED FOR

- ✓ TABLETS
- ✓ WHITEBOARDS
- ✓ COMPUTERS
- ✓ AND MUCH MORE!

Published by Smartbook Media Inc. 350 5th Avenue, 59th Floor New York, NY 10118
Website: www.openlightbox.com

012018
120517

Library of Congress Control Number: 2017960149

ISBN 978-1-5105-3630-2 (hardcover)
ISBN 978-1-5105-3631-9 (multi-user eBook)

Printed in the Brainerd, Minnesota, United States
1 2 3 4 5 6 7 8 9 0 22 21 20 19 18

First published by Cherry Lake in 2014.

Project Coordinator: John Willis
Designer: Ana María Vidal

Every reasonable effort has been made to trace ownership and to obtain permission to reprint copyright material. The publisher would be pleased to have any errors or omissions brought to its attention so that they may be corrected in subsequent printings.

The publisher acknowledges Alamy, Getty Images, Shutterstock, and iStock as the primary image suppliers for this title.